Baccalaureate

Guidelines For Inspirational Worship Services To Honor Graduates

Pamela D. Williams

CSS Publishing Company, Inc., Lima, Ohio

BACCALAUREATE

For more information about CSS Publishing Company resources, visit our website at www.csspub.com or email us at csr@csspub.com or call (800) 241-4056.

Cover design by Barbara Spencer
ISBN-13: 978-0-7880-2526-6
ISBN-10: 0-7880-2526-0   PRINTED IN USA

With all my love
to my husband, Dick,
the one in whom God first planted
the idea of infusing life
in Baccalaureate

Table Of Contents

Preface

How do graduates view the high school Baccalaureate service in your community? Is it an eagerly anticipated event that has the town buzzing the next day? Or does it seem uninspired and outdated, in dire need of an extreme spiritual makeover?

No one wants to waste this precious opportunity to influence the lives of young people on the threshold of impacting our world. However, every year, attendance at high school Baccalaureate services declines.

Why is that?

Some students are unfamiliar with the word "Baccalaureate," except as it refers to an undergraduate degree. They may not know that it also means a worship service specifically designed to honor graduates. Others have heard from previous classes that Baccalaureate is long, boring, and irrelevant. Students and parents alike understandably want to find other ways to spend a beautiful late-spring evening.

Surprisingly, in the three Pennsylvania school districts where my husband and I have ministered, student and family attendance at Baccalaureate services has steadily increased! What is different in these districts?

All it takes is a little creativity, cooperation, and advance preparation. Baccalaureate can become a greatly anticipated event and an effective tool to open the spiritual hearts of all in attendance, infusing them with the love and power of God.

Included in this resource for pastors, ministeriums, and parochial schools are:

- past traditions and current trends in Baccalaureate,
- suggestions for advertising and funding,
- sample letters of invitation,
- student, faculty, and ministerial involvement,
- recommended time line for Baccalaureate preparations,
- order of worship,
- bulletin outline,

- suggestions for hymns, scripture songs, and special music,
- four five-minute meditations,
- two senior-led talks,
- Baccalaureate gift ideas, and
- reception guidelines.

With long-range planning, and input from students as well as sponsors, graduates can walk away from Baccalaureate with spiritual food for thought, wondering in pleased amazement that the service could be over so soon! May God use the suggestions shared here to help you develop a truly inspirational worship experience specifically geared for today's seniors.

Introduction

Those of us in the baby-boomer generation remember Baccalaureate as a long, drawn out, and boring affair. Usually, a well-intentioned preacher spoke at length and, although attendance may have been mandatory, no one could mandate the student's attention.

Previously, Baccalaureate was sponsored and arranged by school officials. However, in 1995, the US Secretary of Education sent every public school superintendent in the United States a statement of principles titled *Religious Expression in Public Schools*. Guidelines within this document restrict the school districts from providing a religious service for seniors graduating from public schools. With the responsibility for this worship opportunity resting, by default, on the shoulders of the community, some school districts suffered a hiatus in Baccalaureate due to a lack of organization.

Presently, many local ecumenical ministeriums sponsor Baccalaureate for the public high school students. Attendance is strictly voluntary and most are poorly attended. Considering that Baccalaureate may be the only church service some of these young people attend, it is imperative that this precious opportunity not be sloughed over. Perhaps this worship service will be the Spirit-opened tug on their hearts that the Lord uses to draw a family into church and ultimately into a personal relationship with him. Share the message of Christ boldly!

Parochial schools, however, retain the freedom to host Baccalaureate on their own terms. Even in this setting, most administrators and students alike are seeking a fresh approach to the time-honored tradition. Private educational facilities will find many suggestions in this resource that will revitalize their worship service for graduates.

In this age of instantaneous stimuli, Baccalaureate also needs to be fast-paced and positive in order to maximize its effectiveness. To that end, this resource includes five-minute meditations, upbeat songs, and creative movement within the service. A little thought and planning to ensure smooth transitions will produce a seamless and meaningful event for everyone involved.

The material in this resource is intended for creating a Christian worship service for graduates and would not be suitable for a multi-faith celebration.

Time Line For Baccalaureate Preparations

A meaningful Baccalaureate service does not just fall together on its own but requires advance planning and most importantly, prayer. Without the blessings of our heavenly Father, all our efforts are meaningless, so let prayer be the balm that bathes all aspects of this event.

Four Months Ahead

- Request the date of Baccalaureate from the school. If the administration does not set a date for it, the sponsoring group should chose a day near graduation, often a Sunday.
- Decide on a location and request permission to use the building. If no area church can accommodate the crowd and no private or community facility such as the YMCA is available, the local high school can be rented. A written rental agreement with the district will need to be completed and approved. Arrangements will also need to be made for a janitor or maintenance person to be present the evening of the service.

Three Months Ahead

- Meet with the class officers or other student representatives to gather their input for Baccalaureate. Let them know that the committee will need their preferences for special music, hymns and praise songs, and student and faculty participants by next month.
- Distribute the informational letter to the senior class, unless it is to be included with the formal invitation.
- Contact musicians for the service. Remember, graduation is an extremely busy time of year for many people.
- Complete a walk-through of the site to be used for Baccalaureate. This can be very beneficial for planning purposes. Stage or altar set up, sound system availability, seating arrangements, and general layout can be assessed.

- Order any gifts to be presented to the graduating students, such as candles, crosses, or Bibles. The school can provide an estimate of how many twelfth-graders will be graduating. Large orders often need to be placed very early to ensure that they will arrive in time for the service.

Two Months Ahead
- If desired, contact the Gideons about distributing Bibles.
- Meet again with student representatives to gather their recommendations.
- Contact those who have been chosen to deliver the meditations.
- Inform the musicians of the hymns and praise songs that have been selected in order to insure the highest quality performance possible.
- Mail a letter to the local pastors inviting them to participate in the service and asking them to promote Baccalaureate to the seniors within their churches. Also request that they solicit helpers for the event.
- Choose a chairperson for the reception who will form a separate reception committee made up of parents or volunteers from the local churches.

Six Weeks Ahead
- Mail formal invitations to the students and their families, informing them of the plans for Baccalaureate.
- Promote Baccalaureate through the local media, including newspapers, radio, and television stations.
- Place a letter or formal invitation to Baccalaureate in the school mailboxes of each member of the faculty and administration.

One Month Ahead
- Finalize the order of worship and distribute parts.
- Check in with the musicians on any concerns or needs they may have.

- Order floral arrangements for the altar and the carnations for the Bouquet Of Thanks.
- Contact volunteers to be ushers for Baccalaureate.
- Arrange for sound and media operators.
- Recruit volunteers to be servers for the reception.
- Order cakes from the bakery or contact people to bake cookies or cakes.

One Week Ahead
- Print a reminder in the newspaper, place announcements on the radio, or send home a colorful note distributed via representatives from the class. In the hectic last week before graduation, even Baccalaureate can slip by the families of graduates, despite their best intentions.
- Check in with the reception chair, the musicians, the student participants, and those giving the meditations.
- Confirm arrangements for early access to the building and any facility set-up requirements.
- Purchase refreshments and paper products for the reception.

Several Hours Before The Baccalaureate Service
- Be sure the doors are opened early.
- Musicians should set up their equipment and complete sound checks.
- Arrange the altar area, including flowers, gifts, candles, and so forth.
- If needed, have balloons, cakes, and flowers delivered.
- Decorate and set up the reception area.
- Give instructions to the ushers and provide them with the bulletins.
- Gather together as many volunteers and musicians as possible and pray for the service.

Student Participation

Student representation in planning a worship service for graduates strengthens the connection between the class and the Baccalaureate sponsors and brings fresh ideas to the board. In some schools, the class officers provide input to the Baccalaureate Committee. In others, pastors from the various local churches invite interested seniors from their congregations to form a group to represent the senior class.

It is also advantageous for seniors to see their peers helping to lead the worship service. This lessens the feeling that the class members are merely spectators and effectively draws them into participation. Selected seniors can read scripture, lead prayers, and introduce the "Bouquet Of Thanks."

Choral or instrumental groups from the school often will eagerly provide special music. This is a prime opportunity for underclassmen to catch a glimpse of just how meaningful Baccalaureate can be.

Some schools elect class chaplains. A very brief, encouraging spiritual word from the chaplain can also be incorporated into the order of worship.

Sample Informational Letter To Local Pastors

Area clergy from the local churches should receive an informal letter inviting them to participate in the Baccalaureate Service. Students appreciate seeing the familiar face of their pastor during the interactive portions of the evening. Pastors can also encourage the graduating students and parents from their churches to attend the event and can enlist volunteers to assist with the service and reception.

Dear Pastor,

It is with great pleasure that the (sponsoring group) is sponsoring the Baccalaureate Service in honor of the (year) Graduating Class of (high school). The service will be held in (location) on (date), beginning at (time).

The program will be a special commissioning service compiled by members of the Graduating Class and the Baccalaureate Committee. We will be presenting each attending senior with several gifts as mementos of this service.

We also will be hosting a reception for all those in attendance following the Baccalaureate Service in the (location). Light refreshments will be served.

The Baccalaureate Committee met with the senior class officers. Guest speakers have been chosen and the order of worship has been planned. (Pianist, praise team) will be providing the music for the evening.

Each pastor in the ministerium is encouraged to attend and participate in the Baccalaureate Service. We need each of you to help make this service as meaningful as possible. Are you willing to be involved? Please contact (contact person, including email address and phone number) by (date).

Please encourage those seniors and their parents who are connected with your church to attend the Baccalaureate Service. This will be an exciting service specifically designed for young people by young people.

We would love to have a few volunteers from each church assist with the service and reception. Please contact (contact person, including email address and phone number) with the names and contact information of those people from your church who are willing to help. If your church would also like to contribute in a monetary form, checks may be made payable to (organization that will be handling the finances for the event).

Thank you for your time and cooperation in this ministry. Seldom do we have such an opportunity to share the love of Christ with so many young men and women who will be impacting our world. Please keep the Baccalaureate Service in your prayers.

In His Service,
The Baccalaureate Committee of
(name of sponsoring group)

Sample Letter Of Invitation To Faculty And Administrators

Faculty members and administrators of the local high school should receive an invitation to Baccalaureate. These fine educators have given much of their time, talents, and energies to the members of the graduating class and have played a large role in their success and achievements. The invitation can be in the form of a letter such as this one or as a formal invitation.

Dear Faculty Members and Administrators,

It is with great pleasure that the (name of sponsoring group) is sponsoring the Baccalaureate Service in honor of the (year) Graduating Class of (name of high school). The service will be held in (location) on (date), beginning at (time).

The program will be a special commissioning service compiled by members of the Graduating Class and the Baccalaureate Committee. We will be presenting each attending senior with several gifts as mementos of this service.

We also will be hosting a reception for all those in attendance following the Baccalaureate Service in the (location). Light refreshments will be served.

We would be honored by your attendance at the Baccalaureate Service and Reception. You have played a large role in the success and achievements of these young people. Please join us in celebrating this great accomplishment with the students and in asking God's blessing on each one of them.

In His Service,
The Baccalaureate Committee of
(name of sponsoring group)

Sample Informational Letter To Seniors

Most times, only one mailing is sent to the seniors and their families. Sometimes the students on the Baccalaureate Committee will hand out an informational letter at a class meeting about three months before Baccalaureate. In other situations, the informational letter is included as an insert with the formal invitation. If an insert with the formal invitation is chosen, present it in an aesthetically pleasing way, printed on a half sheet of quality paper.

Dear Senior, Parents, and Family Members,

With great pleasure the (sponsoring group) is sponsoring a Baccalaureate Service in honor of the (year) Graduating Class of (high school). The service will be held in (location) on (date), beginning at (time).

The members of the senior class will have an active part in Baccalaureate. The program will be a special commissioning service complied by members of the class and the Baccalaureate Committee. (Sponsoring group) will be presenting each attending senior with several gifts as mementos of this service.

We also will be hosting a reception for all those in attendance following the Baccalaureate Service in the (location). Light refreshments will be served.

This will be an event that is organized with you, the senior, in mind, and we would be honored by your presence. If you or your parents have any questions, you can contact (contact person, including email address and phone number).

Thank you so much for your time and consideration in this matter. We look forward to seeing you on (date).

> In His Service,
> The Baccalaureate Committee of
> (name of sponsoring group)

Sample Formal Invitation

A formal invitation to Baccalaureate should be printed on substantial cardstock and if possible, mailed to each student and their families. In some public school districts, students give written permission at the beginning of the year to release their mailing address to pre-approved groups. If available, ask for a copy of these addresses to mail the invitations.

In those districts where no addresses are available, publish a Baccalaureate invitation in the local newspaper or submit an article describing the service and inviting the students, their families, faculty members, and administrators to the event. Broadcast the same information on the community bulletin board of local radio and television stations.

As an alternative to the letter of invitation to the faculty and administration, this same formal invitation could be printed and placed in their school mailboxes.

A sample formal invitation can be seen on the next page.

(Sponsoring Group)
invites you
to a
Baccalaureate Service
honoring the
(High School)
Graduating Class of (Year)
on
(Date)
at
(Time)
in the
(Location)
(Room)
(City, State)
Seniors will gather at (Time) in the (Location).

A reception with light refreshments will be served
in the (Location)
immediately following the service.

Sample Press Release
For Local Newspapers

(Sponsoring group) will be sponsoring a Baccalaureate Service in honor of the (year) Graduating Class of (high school). The service will be held in (location) on (date), beginning at (time).

All graduating seniors of (high school) and their families and guests are invited to attend. The faculty and administration are also encouraged to be present for this celebration.

This will be an exciting service specifically designed for young people by young people. The program will be a special commissioning service compiled by members of the Class of (year) and the (sponsoring group) Baccalaureate Committee. This will be an event that is organized with the students in mind, and members of the graduating class will have an active part. Each senior attending will be presented with several gifts as mementos of the service.

Immediately following the Baccalaureate Service, there will be a reception in the (location). Light refreshments will be served.

The Baccalaureate Committee welcomes all area pastors to participate in this great opportunity to share the love of Christ with so many young men and women who will be impacting our world.

Volunteers are also needed to assist with the service and reception. Churches and individuals who would like to contribute monetarily may make checks payable to (organization that will be handling the finances for the event).

Anyone having questions about Baccalaureate and those wishing to volunteer may contact (contact person, including email address and phone number).

Sample Public Service Announcements For Radio And Television

Radio

Please keep in mind that the deadline to submit announcements to radio stations is three to four weeks before the event.

60-Second Announcement

A Baccalaureate Service in honor of the (year) Graduating Class of (high school) will be held at (location) on (date), at (time). All graduating seniors of (high school) and their families and guests are invited to attend this exciting event designed by youth for youth. Music for the evening will be provided by (name) of (church or hometown).

Immediately following the Baccalaureate Service, there will be a reception in the (location). The Baccalaureate Committee also welcomes the (high school) faculty and administration. All area pastors are encouraged to participate. Volunteers are needed to assist with the service and reception.

Anyone having questions about Baccalaureate and those wishing to contribute or volunteer may contact (contact person, including email address and phone number).

30-Second Announcement

All (high school) seniors and their guests are invited to attend a Baccalaureate Service honoring the Class of (year) at (location) on (date), at (time). Immediately following the service, there will be a reception in the (location). Anyone having questions about Baccalaureate or wishing to contribute or volunteer may contact (contact person, including email address and phone number).

Television

Please keep in mind that the deadline to submit announcements to most community access television stations is three to four weeks before the event.

Announcement For Community Access Television
Events Calendar
(high school) Class of (year)
Baccalaureate Service
(location)
(date and time)
For more information
(phone number)

Order Of Worship
With Explanations

The following order of worship for Baccalaureate has repeatedly proven successful. It is offered here simply as an example and can easily be varied. The welcome, prayers, introductions, and blessing may be read as printed or personalized to suit the needs of the sponsoring organization. One person acting as the Master of Ceremonies could introduce each part of the service, the speakers, and the musicians. As an alternative, stage directions are included, beginning with the Welcome, for each speaker to introduce the next event. Use whichever option will provide the most seamless worship flow.

A sample Baccalaureate bulletin and suggested music are also included in this publication.

Prelude
(The prelude can be pre-recorded music, a pianist, an organist, or a praise band, depending on the preferences of the Baccalaureate Committee and students.)

Welcome
(Welcome may be given by a pastor or other member of the sponsoring group.)

Good evening! The Baccalaureate Committee would like to extend a special welcome to the senior class and their families and friends. We also welcome teachers, administrators, and clergy. This service of celebration has been planned entirely with the seniors in mind. We invite you to stand as the graduating class processes in at this time.

Processional
(Students process in carrying their lighted candles to special music.)

Placement Of Candles
(Students place the lighted candles on the altar area. They should then be seated either in a reserved section at the front of the auditorium or sanctuary or on the stage.)

Opening Prayer
(The opening prayer can be shared by a student, pastor, or other member of the sponsoring group.)

Father, we thank you for helping each of these young adults to accomplish this educational milestone. Lord, may all that is said and done this evening be a blessing to those gathered here and may it open the door for you to impact each life. Amen.

Let us join in singing our first hymn, (song title) located (where printed).

Hymn Or Praise Song
(If hymnals are unavailable, words to all the songs should be either printed as bulletin inserts or projected on a screen at the appropriate time.)

Scripture
(Scripture should be read by one of the seniors. The reader will need the scripture several weeks in advance of the service, printed in the version that the meditation speaker prefers, so that they may practice sufficiently.)

Please be seated. I will be reading from the book of (book of the Bible), chapter (chapter number), verses (verses selected).

Meditation

Special Music
(The special music could be introduced by the person who has just given the meditation.)

Scripture Challenge
(Can be given by the class chaplain or another senior.)

Lord's Prayer
(Can be lead by the class chaplain, another student, a pastor, or other member of the sponsoring group. Printing out the prayer will avoid stumbling over "debts" or "trespasses.")

Please pray with me the words Jesus taught his disciples.

Our Father in heaven, holy is your name. May your kingdom come, your will be done on earth as in heaven. Give us today our daily bread. Forgive us our sins as we forgive those who sin against us. Save us from the time of trial and deliver us from evil. For the kingdom, the power, and the glory are yours, now and forever. Amen.

Bouquet Of Thanks With Musical Accompaniment
(To be lead by a senior.)

Hymn Or Praise Song
(Should be introduced by the senior reading the scripture.)

Let us join in singing (song title) found in (location).

Scripture
(Scripture should be read by one of the seniors. The reader will need the scripture several weeks in advance of the service, printed in the version that the meditation speaker prefers, so that they may practice sufficiently.)

Please be seated. I will be reading from the book of (book of the Bible), chapter (chapter number), verses (verses selected).

Meditation

Presentation Of Gifts With Musical Accompaniment
(Should be introduced by a pastor or other member of the sponsoring group. If present, the Gideons may also wish to say a few words before the gifts are presented.)

Tonight each of the graduates will be receiving a (list gift[s]) as a symbol(s) of faith. Seniors, as you come forward, please give your name to one of the pastors, so that they may share a brief prayer with you. May the prayer and the gifts serve as a reminder of God's presence with you wherever your path may lead.

Hymn Or Praise Song

(The pastor who will be leading the benediction could introduce this hymn.)

Please stand as we sing our closing number, (song title) found in (location).

Benediction/Blessing

(Lead by a pastor.)

Please join me in extending our hands toward the students and praying the blessing printed before you.

The Lord bless you and keep you: the Lord make his face to shine upon you, and be gracious to you, the Lord lift up his countenance upon you, and give you peace. Amen.

At this time seniors are invited to come up and take a candle from the altar and recess back up the aisle. We would like to invite everyone to join us for a reception in the (location) immediately following the service.

Recessional

(The recessional can be pre-recorded music, a pianist, an organist, or a praise band, depending on the preferences of the Baccalaureate Committee and students.)

About The Bulletins

Often families will save a bulletin as a keepsake of Baccalaureate. If plain paper is used for the bulletin, be sure to choose a heavier weight and make the cover design attractive. Graduation bulletins with beautiful pre-printed covers are available from local and online suppliers such as CSS Publishing Company, Concordia, Cokesbury, and Christian Book Distributors.

Whichever type of bulletin is chosen, personalize it with the name of the school and the date of the service. Also include the titles of the songs, the musicians' names, the names and positions or titles of the speakers and readers (such as Reverend Ed Park, York UMC or Judy Rosen, Class President), and, if necessary, include directions for procedures.

The bulletin is also an excellent venue for expressing gratitude for all those who made the evening possible. List the florist, bakery, churches, and others who have contributed significantly to the success of the event.

When the entire worship service and announcements are projected on a screen, bulletins may not be necessary, except as a memento. Projecting some parts of the service, for instance, like the words to the songs, while printing other parts, is also an option to consider.

Sample Bulletin

(High School)
Class of (Year)
Baccalaureate Service
(Date)
(Time)
(Location)

Prelude	(song title, musician)
Welcome	(speaker)
Processional	(song title)
Placement Of Candles	
Opening Prayer	(speaker)
Hymn Or Praise Song	(song title)
Scripture	(reader)
Meditation	(speaker)
Special Music	(song title, musician)
Scripture Challenge	(reader)

Lord's Prayer
Our Father in heaven, holy is your name. May your kingdom come, your will be done on earth as in heaven. Give us today our daily bread. Forgive us our sins as we forgive those who sin against us. Save us from the time of trial and deliver us from evil. For the kingdom, the power, and the glory are yours, now and forever. Amen.

Bouquet Of Thanks	(speaker)
With Musical Accompaniment	(song title)

Hymn Or Praise Song	(song title)

Scripture	(reader)

Meditation	(speaker)

Presentation Of Gifts	(speaker)
With Musical Accompaniment	(song title)

Hymn Or Praise Song	(song title)

Benediction/Blessing (speaker)

The Lord bless you and keep you: the Lord make his face to shine upon you, and be gracious to you, the Lord lift up his countenance upon you, and give you peace. Amen.

Recessional (song title)

We would like to invite everyone to attend a reception in the (location) immediately following the service.

Our special thanks to (florist, bakery, and so on).

Music For Baccalaureate

Music adds so much to any special occasion, touching the heart when words just are not enough. The first few notes of a song can trigger a flashback of memories to a specific moment in time. One of the aims for Baccalaureate is to choose music that will create such an experience for the graduates.

The decision of whether the service will follow a contemporary or traditional style should be made with the input of the students involved in the planning. Give special consideration to their requests for songs and hymns. Keep in mind that in a public school setting, it is also important to choose well-known songs that cross denominational boundaries.

A pianist, organist, praise team, or band could accompany the hymns and choruses that will be sung during Baccalaureate, as well as performing the songs for the rest of the service. As an alternative, special music by individual teens or school choral groups is always greatly appreciated by those in attendance. People love hearing the extraordinary abilities of familiar, local talent.

Compact discs could be played for the Processional, the Bouquet Of Thanks, the Giving Of Gifts, or the Recessional. However, the arrangements chosen need to allow enough time for all the graduates to participate and return to their seats.

Varying combinations of these musical options creates an interesting and enjoyable evening. A pianist could accompany hymns, a praise team could lead choruses, and a soloist and student choral group could provide the special numbers.

If Baccalaureate is held in a church, hymnals will be readily available. When printing or projecting words to hymns or choruses, a Christian Copyright Licensing International (CCLI) number will need to be noted.

God can speak through a variety of styles of music. Be open to his leading. Along with the expected emphasis of Christian music, secular songs with a powerfully positive message can speak to the students. Vocal or instrumental versions of these pieces work especially well for those parts of the service where performance songs are needed, such as the Processional, the Giving Of Gifts, or during the distribution of the Bouquet Of Thanks. Just to get the creative juices flowing, a few appropriate song titles are suggested below.

Processional
"Keep The Candle Burning" by Point of Grace
"A Whole New World" by Menken and Rice
"Faith Of The Heart" by Diane Warren
"Lift High The Cross" by Kitchin and Nicholson

Hymns
"Amazing Grace" by John Newton
"Here I Am, Lord" by Daniel L. Schutte
"Hymn Of Promise" by Natalie Sleeth
"Stepping In The Light" by Eliza Hewitt

Praise Songs
"Shine, Jesus, Shine" by Graham Kendrick
"Step By Step" by Beaker
"Open The Eyes Of My Heart" by Paul Baloche
"Shout To The Lord" by Darlene Zschech

Bouquet Of Thanks
"Wind Beneath My Wings" by Bette Midler
"Thank You, Lord" by Don Moen
"Thank You, Lord" by Ricky Nelson
"Thank You" by The Katinas

Gift Distribution
"Above All" by Lenny LeBlanc and Paul Baloche
"Thy Word" by Amy Grant
"God Of Wonders" by Marc Byrd and Steve Hindalong
"How Great Thou Art" by Carol Boberg

Recessional

"Pray For Me" by Michael W. Smith

"The River" by Garth Brooks

"Go Light Your World" by Chris Rice

"Go My Children With My Blessing" by Jaroslav Vajda

Bouquet Of Thanks

One especially touching moment recommended for the Baccalaureate service is the Bouquet Of Thanks. Bouquets of loose carnations in the school colors should flank each side of the stage or altar area, with at least one carnation for each graduate. Local florists are usually delighted to provide carnations at cost for Baccalaureate. The favor can be returned by a simple acknowledgment to them in the bulletin.

At the appointed moment in the worship service, one senior, representing all of the graduates, will share a few words of heartfelt thanks for those parents, loved ones, educators, or others who have helped them reach this momentous occasion in their lives. While special music plays, the students come forward, pick out a carnation, and deliver it to the person in the audience whose influence they would like to recognize.

This simple expression of gratitude is often the highlight of the entire service, both for the students and for those receiving their thanks. Careful choice of the music played during this time can add immensely to the ambiance of the moment.

To introduce the Bouquet Of Thanks, the appointed student could share the following or something similar:

Family, friends, teachers, although we don't often take the time or the effort to express our gratitude, the seniors here tonight feel we owe a special thank you to many people who have helped us to reach this milestone in our lives. The bouquet of carnations is given to the glory of God in honor of all those people who have encouraged and supported us along the way. We want you to know that in our hearts we are truly thankful and we love you very much. At this time, each senior is invited to present a carnation to someone here as a symbol of their thanks for all those who played a part in the accomplishment of their goal. If that special someone couldn't make it this evening, seniors may take a carnation following the service and present it to the special person at a later time.

Scripture Challenge

Some schools elect a class chaplain along with their other class officers. Baccalaureate is an excellent opportunity for the chaplain to encourage the other members of the class with some uplifting and challenging words from scripture.

If the class does not have a chaplain, a senior chosen by the Baccalaureate Committee could offer the scripture challenge. An example of a brief message follows.

As a senior (and class chaplain), I would like to share two scriptures that will be helpful to us as we begin a new adventure in our lives. The first comes from Jeremiah 29:11, where God says:

> *I alone know the plans I have for you, plans to bring you prosperity and not disaster, plans to bring about the future you hope for. Then you will call to me. You will come and pray to me, and I will answer you. You will seek me, and you will find me because you will seek me with all your heart.* (TEV)

This scripture assures us that God has a plan for us, even if some of our futures may be "undeclared" at the moment. He knows what is best and how to make it happen. We need to line up our plans with his plans by seeking God with all of our hearts.

The second scripture I would like to share is a challenge from 1 Timothy 4:12. The apostle Paul said these words to a young man named Timothy:

> *Do not let anyone look down on you because you are young, but be an example for the believers in your speech, your conduct, your love, faith, and purity.* (TEV)

Sometimes we hear people say things like "You're too young to know any better," or "Hey, I'm just a kid!" But the Bible challenges young people to be a good example to others. God gives us the power to resist the temptation to conform to the ways and habits of the world. This scripture encourages us to show the difference God makes in our lives by how we talk, act, think, feel, and believe.

May God bless each one of us as we now go out into the world and do our best to make it a better place.

About The Meditations

The meditations for Baccalaureate offer a wonderful opportunity to share the teachings of Jesus with the young men and women of the graduating class. The keys to a memorable address are enthusiastic, committed speakers with very brief messages, strictly limited to five to seven minutes each.

Two ministers could each preach a very short sermon, or two faculty members could speak, especially in a parochial school setting. Graduates always appreciate hearing a teacher share their faith. However, public school administration policy on staff and faculty participation in, or collaboration with, a non-school based group that organizes or schedules a Baccalaureate Service varies from state to state and from district to district. Check with your local administrator. Asking one teacher and one pastor to speak not only provides a nice balance, but also brings the advantage of differing perspectives.

It is important not to assume that people are familiar with the Bible. According to church growth and evangelism statistics, 50% of the population is totally unchurched or attends church less than five times per year. Knowing this should affect not only the sermon content, but also the introduction of the scripture readings and the wording for prayers. Avoid language that excludes seekers and is meaningful only to those who have been raised in the church.

Four meditations are included in this resource and may be used as is or personalized as needed.

Sample Meditation:
Dispelling The Darkness

The Bible says in John 8:12, "Again Jesus spoke to them, saying, 'I am the light of the world. Whoever follows me will never walk in darkness but will have the light of life.' "

Graduates, as we gathered before the start of the service, all of you were given candles, which you placed on the altar area. If we now turned out the lights, the glow from these candles would easily illuminate this stage, making it safe to walk around up here. Lots of obstacles might trip us if it were dark, but because of the candlelight, we could avoid walking off the edge or stumbling over power cords or running into the table.

In the same way, we all occasionally experience times in our lives that we consider "dark" — times of uncertainty, anger, hurt, and loss. We need someone to shed light on our problems and dispel our fears, someone to help us sort things out and indicate the best way to turn. Groping around in the dark can be frightening and dangerous.

In the scripture that was read, Jesus refers to himself as the light of the world. He promises that we will never walk in darkness. When we have him with us, he sheds light on our path and shows us the way to go. He helps us to see the way through difficult circumstances. No matter how dark things may seem, he can bring light to the situation.

But there is a condition that accompanies this promise. Did you catch it?

"Whoever follows me will never walk in darkness...." In order for Jesus to shine his light on our lives we must be following him. Following....

Most of us can remember a night when a storm knocked out the power and we had to follow someone carrying a candle or shining a flashlight in the darkness. If we veered away from them, we found ourselves in the dark. If we tried to run ahead, we exceeded the reach of their light. But as long as we stayed close and followed them, their flashlight or candle lit the way and illuminated the path for us.

Let's look at the scripture again. "Whoever follows me will never walk in darkness but will have the light of life." Are we following Jesus? Or are we trying to run ahead of him, seeking our own path and insisting on our own way? Are we staying beside him, letting his light lead us? Or have we gotten sidetracked, pouring all our time and energy into the pleasures and challenges this world has to offer?

Have you ever been working on something that was difficult to see when someone stood in your light? Maybe you were trying to take the knot out of a necklace or were searching for a lost item. The person blocking your light produced shadows that made it impossible to continue.

Similarly, spiritual obstacles — like mixed-up priorities, questionable influences, or sheer busyness — can interfere with our relationship with Jesus. As a result, we find ourselves groping our way through life without the benefit of Jesus' light shining in our lives.

In Matthew 28:20, Jesus promises that he will always be with us. No matter what difficulties we may have to go through, no matter what challenges we may have to face, we are not alone. Simply by following Jesus, we can have the comfort and guidance of his light.

How do we go about following him? First, we need to get to know him better by reading the Bible and talking to others who know him. Second, we need to talk directly to him — asking him to lead us. We call this prayer. Third, we need to follow his example. First Peter 2:21 says that Christ left us an example that we might follow in his steps.

Our prayer for you this evening is that the candle you will take with you as you leave the auditorium will serve as a reminder to follow Jesus and allow him to light your path.

Sample Meditation:
The Clean Slate

In 2 Corinthian 5:17 we read, "Therefore, if anyone is in Christ, he is a new creation; the old has gone, the new has come!" (NIV).

Seniors, this week you will be graduating from high school and commencing a new phase of your life. Some of you will attend college or technical school. Others will join a branch of the military, while still others will begin a full-time job. No matter what your plans may be, this is a time of fresh starts, new beginnings, and deeper commitments.

Leaving well-known hangouts, friends, and routines behind can be a bittersweet moment. The unknown looms ahead. New experiences may seem confusing. Unfamiliar faces and places can be a bit intimidating.

However, all of us also have incidents and mistakes in our lives that we are anxious to leave behind. We want to forget them and we want everyone else to forget them, too. Therefore, many of us actually look forward to a fresh start. We are excited about embarking on a new life, a second chance, a clean slate!

The scripture passage that was read speaks about a time when the old life passes away and we are given a new life. When does this change take place? Is it when we graduate, get married, or have children?

While all of those are highly significant moments, the scripture is referring to a spiritual event. The opening phrase, "if anyone is in Christ," clues us in to the type of change that is meant here. This is the transforming decision to totally commit our lives to Christ.

In a short time each of you will be given a cross as a keepsake of this special service of dedication. Why was a cross chosen as a gift for you? Traditionally, a cross symbolizes the Christian faith. It recalls the sacrifice that our Savior Jesus Christ made for us. When Christ died on the cross, all humanity reached a vital turning point. From that moment on, the old barriers between God and humankind were torn down and a new relationship was born. Now all that is required for us to receive a second chance, a clean slate, is to put our faith in Christ — to truly believe that he paid the price to wash away all our sins.

In 2 Corinthians 5:17, we are promised that if we are "in Christ" our old ways are forgiven and forgotten and we are given a new beginning. But what does it really mean to be "in Christ"? How do we do that?

Consider this: Most of us have gone swimming a few times in our lives. How many of us know how to float? Can we float if we only go into the water up to our ankles? No! How about up to our knees? No way! Is waist deep, deep enough? No! It is only when we are totally submerged that the water will hold us up. If we flounder around trying to touch bottom, we can't float. We have to relax and let the water buoy us up.

Likewise, to be "in Christ" we must totally give ourselves to him. We cannot just add a little of Christ to our already crowded lives. We must let go of our own wants and desires and give him total control. At that point, we are submerged in him and he will make us a new creation.

When you receive your cross this evening, it is our prayer that, as you face these days of new beginnings in your life, you will take this opportunity to start anew spiritually, also. May the cross remind you of the clean slate and the new life that Christ offers to all of us, if we will just commit our whole selves to him.

Sample Meditation:
Light For Our World

Jesus tells us, in Matthew 5:14-16, "You are the light of the world. A city built on a hill cannot be hid. No one after lighting a lamp puts it under the bushel basket, but on the lampstand, and it gives light to all in the house. In the same way, let your light shine before others, so that they may see your good works and give glory to your Father in heaven."

One of the gifts you have received tonight is a candle. Today, we use candles to set a mood, create a holiday atmosphere, or to perfume the air. However, during the time of Jesus and throughout history, candles were essential for carrying out day-to-day routines. Candles provided light to read by and showed what lay ahead. They helped to dispel fear and to warn of danger. Candlelight revealed obstacles and indicated the safe path. Even today, the lighting of a candle continues to welcome people home, provide comfort, and, in churches, remind of us of the presence of Jesus.

In the scripture passage that was read, Jesus tells us that we — those of us who follow him — are like light — like a candle — for the whole world. You are about to take a new path on your life's journey. As you venture out beyond these well-known walls and the security of family and friends, you can be a candle for the world.

"How?" you ask.

In John 8:12 we read, "Again Jesus spoke to them, saying, 'I am the light of the world. Whoever follows me will never walk in darkness but will have the light of life.' " When we draw close to Jesus, our lives are filled with light. Like a streetlight attracts moths, the light of Jesus shining through us beckons to those who are struggling.

Why is that?

When we live for Jesus we have him as a guide for us. When we face uncertainty, we are never alone. He is always there to whisper, "This is the path to follow." When we live for Jesus, we have the Bible to help us discern what is right from what is wrong, what is safe from what is dangerous. When we live for Jesus, we have the comfort of his Spirit constantly with us when we are frightened or hurting.

At one time or another, everyone goes through trying times and challenges — times when we feel confused about what to do, unsure of where to turn, and fearful of what lies ahead. Often we will turn to a friend who seems to have peace in the midst of life's storms, a friend who has made wise choices, a friend who treats them with compassion. Like a candle that shows the way in the darkness, how we live can help point others to God, where they will find the guidance, direction, and security they need.

For the most part, these days we use electric lights or battery-powered flashlights. It's so easy to flick on a switch, and voila, we have light! But a candle is what we fall back on when there is no other source of power. During the good times in their lives, people may not notice that we live differently. Like batteries, they can operate under their own power. It is during those stormy times of life, when they will need a candle in the darkness — someone to turn to who can direct them to the real source of power — Jesus. Each one of us can be that person — that light — shining before them and ultimately pointing them to the Light that illuminates our own path.

Sample Meditation:
Becoming A Follower

In Mark 8:34, we read, "[Jesus] called the crowd with his disciples, and said to them, 'If any want to become my followers, let them deny themselves and take up their cross and follow me.' "

Many of us wear gold or silver cross-shaped earrings or necklaces just like this one. *(Wear a necklace with a large cross pendant or hold one out for the audience to see.)* In fact, this evening all of you seniors will be receiving a cross necklace during the worship service.

Crosses are quite a common ornament today. Couples receive decorative crosses as wedding gifts. During the Easter season, lily-covered crosses adorn windows and doors and we even see cross-shaped chocolates. Churches place numerous brass and polished wood crosses throughout their worship areas.

But what does a cross really symbolize? What does displaying or wearing a cross say to others about us? Is it merely a beautifully crafted piece?

Though crosses may be ornamental for us, during the time of Jesus they were an instrument of death used for capital punishment. The cross represents Christianity because it is on a cross that Jesus Christ died as payment for our sins. The cross proclaims our Christian faith — our belief in God and commitment to following his Son, Jesus Christ.

In the scripture that was read, Jesus explains his expectations of those who want to be one of his followers. Let's look at it in three parts: 1) deny self, 2) take up the cross, and 3) follow Jesus' example.

First, we need to deny self. Denying self implies waiting, sacrificing, and restraint. We live in an instant world — instant food, instant money, instant messages — and most of us find the discipline of saying no to ourselves too challenging. Often we feel that we deserve to be first, to be accommodated, to have it all. But God has a different outlook. The principles Jesus taught are reinforced

53

throughout the Bible. In chapter 2 of Philippians, we learn that we are not to look to our own interests, but to the interests of others. "The attitude you should have is the one that Christ Jesus had ... of his own free will he gave up all he had and took the nature of a servant" (Philippians 2:5, 7 TEV). Instead of concentrating on making sure our own needs are met, God expects us to put others first.

Second, Jesus asks us to take up our cross. This statement conjures up mental images of picking up something heavy and awkward — of bearing a burden. Galatians 6:2 simply encourages us to "Help carry one another's burdens ..." (TEV). Lightening the load of a friend who is struggling can often mean that we must take on extra responsibilities and challenges ourselves. To do so requires sacrifice on our part — sacrifice of our preferences, our time, and our energies.

Finally, Jesus boldly tells us to follow him. He is our example. Remember the "WWJD" bracelets of a few years back? They asked, "What would Jesus do?" The Bible shares with us that Jesus denied himself, choosing to leave his heavenly home and come to earth and live among us. When Jesus picked up his cross, he took on the burden of our sins, and carried them for us, making the ultimate sacrifice — his life. In John 15:13, Jesus tells us, "No one has greater love than this, to lay down one's life for one's friends." And that is exactly what Jesus did. He loved us enough to offer his life on the cross for us. Though the world may teach us to look out for ourselves, the cross reminds us to live as Jesus lived — putting others first.

In Acts 17:6, those who opposed Christianity claimed that the followers of Jesus were turning the world upside down. As you receive your cross, our hope is that one day others will say that you, too, made a radical difference in the world, as you first, deny yourself, second, help carry another's burdens, and third, follow the example of Jesus.

Gifts For The Seniors

Everyone likes to receive gifts. Keepsakes from special occasions serve as reminders of the event for years to come. Gifts for graduates abound. Local Christian bookstores, companies like CTA Inc. (Christian Tools of Affirmation), and online stores such as Christianbook.com offer meaningful gifts at affordable prices.

Candles are often associated with ceremonies both within the church and in secular venues as they help to create a certain ambiance. Just before processing in, seniors could receive a lighted candle to carry. As part of the processional the candles would be placed on the altar, where the light from the candles would lend a reverence to the service. To conclude the worship experience, the students would take a lighted candle from the altar and recess from the auditorium or sanctuary, symbolizing carrying their light out into the world.

A cross necklace is especially apropos as a remembrance for Baccalaureate. Immediately following a sermon on the cross, all pastors and priests present could come to the front. The students would then approach the clergy of their choice, who would present them with a cross necklace accompanied by a brief personal prayer.

A Bible is another appropriate gift for a graduate. The Gideons always appreciate an opportunity to share God's word. As part of the Baccalaureate Service, a representative from this fine evangelistic organization could present each young man and woman with a New Testament or Bible.

While candles, crosses, and Bibles are mentioned here, they are just a few of the many items available. Gifts specifically geared for graduates vary considerably in purpose as well as cost. Keychains, devotional books, lapel pins, pens, bookmarks, zipper pulls — the list goes on and on, with choices to fit every budget. Whether the gift is simple and inexpensive or elegant and costly, seniors will remember the special worship service planned just for them each time they start their cars, zip their coats, or wear their necklaces.

Reception Guidelines

A reception will allow the participants, families, faculty, clergy, and administration to fellowship with one another and to congratulate the graduates. The committee responsible for the reception should be separate from the committee that plans the worship service. However, frequent communication between the two groups is absolutely necessary.

Choose a chairperson to take charge of the reception. This person will then form a separate reception committee made up of parents or volunteers from the local churches. This group will plan, prepare, decorate, set up, and serve refreshments following the worship experience.

The chair from the reception committee should also contact an official from the venue where the service is to be held. This will aid in coordinating matters such as rooms to be used, time needed for set up, and policies regarding the use of furniture, appliances, and serving dishes. Again, advance planning is vital to the success of the event.

The gathering could take place in the cafeteria, fellowship hall, or a multipurpose room. Refreshments can be as simple as cake or cookies, pretzels, and a beverage. Sheet cakes purchased from a local bakery and decorated in the school colors work well, as do donations of a variety of cakes or cookies solicited from families or local churches.

Decorations and tableware can be as elaborate or as basic as the committee wishes. Flower arrangements from the worship service can be used for the reception, also. Balloons, plastic utensils, table covers, and paper napkins in the school colors are readily available from dollar stores or other discount and paper outlet stores. A festive atmosphere can be created for just a few dollars and a little extra effort.

Funding For Baccalaureate

Financial support for a Baccalaureate Service can be derived from a variety of sources. In parochial schools, Baccalaureate is usually built into the budget for the school, while those sponsoring the service for public high schools must raise their own monetary support.

Funding may come either from the local ministerium treasury or as contributions from individual churches. One church may buy the crosses, while another purchases the candles, and still another provides the punch and cake.

Most churches feel Baccalaureate is an outreach opportunity that is well worth the sacrifice of time, energy, manpower, and money. Some hold fund-raisers specifically for Baccalaureate, such as weekly soup and sandwich luncheons during Lent or monthly pancake breakfasts or spaghetti dinners. The community will eagerly rally behind these meals knowing their children will benefit.

Attempting to do everything in this resource the first year may prove daunting. Although the cost factor should not be allowed to stifle creativity when planning Baccalaureate, choose what seems most meaningful and attainable to begin with and then add different aspects to the event each year.

References

http://www.greenbelt.com/news/97/073135.htm

http://www.ed.gov/Speeches/08-1995/religion.html

http://sundayschool.ag.org/Training_and_Helps/Index

LaVergne, TN USA
11 February 2010
172784LV00004B/37/P